What they don't tell you about

ANCIENT GREEKS

By Bob Fowke

Illustrations by Andrew Mee

This book is *not dedicated* to the Minotaur,
who liked to have lots of young people
sacrificed to himself.

Hallo, my name's *Herakles* (although some people, especially Romans, call me *Hercules*). I'm a legendary hero. All right, so I went mad and killed my wife and children - we all make mistakes. Underneath these muscles I'm a good guy. So if you come with me you'll be in safe hands and I can show you all about the amazing Ancient Greeks. They had to be amazing - after all, I was their hero!

Published in 2013 by Wayland

Text and illustrations
copyright © Bob Fowke 2013

Wayland
338 Euston Road
London NW1 3BH

Wayland Australia
Level 17/207 Kent Street
Sydney, NSW 2000

Produced for Wayland by Bob Fowke & Co
Cover design: Lisa Peacock
Cover illustration: Nick Hardcastle

A CIP catalogue record for this book is available from the British Library.

ISBN 978 0 7502 8050 1

10 9 8 7 6 5 4 3 2 1

Printed and bound by CPI Group (UK) Ltd, Croydon, CR0 4YY

First published in 1998 by Hodder Children's Books

Wayland is a division of Hachette Children's Books, an Hachette UK Company
www.hachette.co.uk

CONTENTS

Watch out for the *Sign of the Foot*! Whenever you see this sign in the book it means there are some more details at the *FOOT* of the page. Like here.

FEELING GREECEY?

SUN, SAND AND STATUES

PASS THE SUNTAN LOTION

Ah! The sun, the sand, the beautiful Mediterranean Sea! Hot in summer, not too cold in winter - the perfect place for a holiday!

RHODES HARBOUR

MEDITERRANEAN SEA

But remember - the Mediterranean Sea was once both highway and battle-trail for the very amazing Ancient Greeks. They lived round its shores like frogs round a pond more than two thousand years ago. Let's step back in time and see Rhodes as the Ancient Greeks would have seen it ...

It was a famous Greek called *Plato* who said that his people lived round the Mediterranean 'like frogs round a pond'. More on him later.

COLOSSAL OR WHAT!

The Ancient Greeks were brilliantly brainy (well, some of them) and awesomely artistic (well, several of them). They built five of the seven wonders of the Ancient World 👣 . Of all these wonders 👣 the most

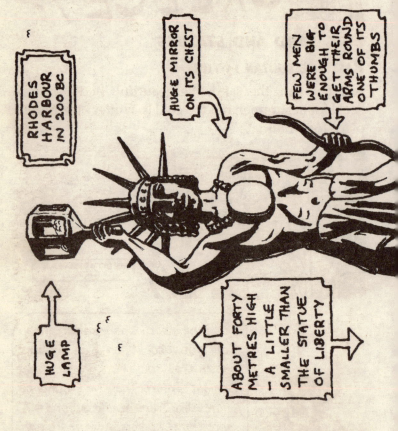

RHODES HARBOUR IN 200 BC

HUGE MIRROR ON ITS CHEST

FEW MEN WERE BIG ENOUGH TO GET THEIR ARMS ROUND ONE OF ITS THUMBS

HUGE LAMP

ABOUT FORTY METRES HIGH — A LITTLE SMALLER THAN THE STATUE OF LIBERTY

👣 *Ancient World* normally means the world before the fall of the Roman Empire around AD 400.

👣 The Colossus of Rhodes, the Mausoleum at Harlicarnasus in modern Turkey, the Temple of Artemis at Ephesus in modern Turkey, the Statue of Zeus at Olympus in Greece and the Pharos lighthouse at Alexandria in Egypt. The two non-Greek wonders were the Pyramids and the Hanging Gardens of Babylon.

awesome of all was the Colossus of Rhodes, a vast statue to *Helios,* the god of the Sun, which stood at the entrance to Rhodes harbour.

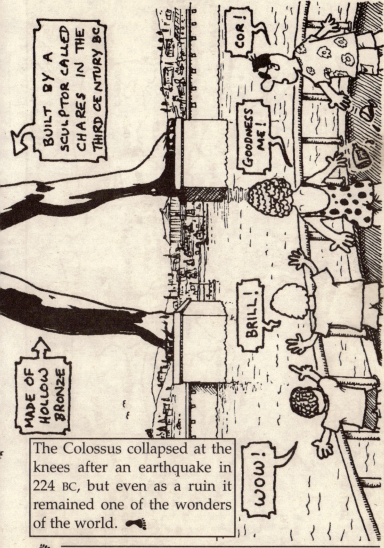

BUILT BY A SCULPTOR CALLED CHARES IN THE THIRD CENTURY BC

MADE OF HOLLOW BRONZE

COR!

GOODNESS ME!

BRILL!

WOW!

The Colossus collapsed at the knees after an earthquake in 224 BC, but even as a ruin it remained one of the wonders of the world.

The broken pieces were finally sold to a Jewish scrap metal dealer in AD 656.

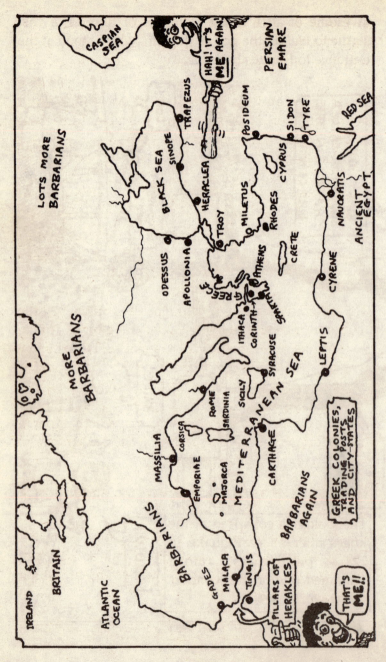

A PLACE BY THE POND

The Greeks lived in small city-states, called *polis*, which is where words like 'police' and 'politics' come from. Each polis was a teeny, tiny country with its own government and laws. Because of war, quarrels or overpopulation at home, or just for adventure, these midget states often started new cities called *colonies* far from home. Because the *colonists* travelled in ships new colonies were usually set up near to the sea. In this way the Greeks spread around the Mediterranean.

The little city-states often fought each other in little midget wars , but being Greek was a bit like being part of one large family. All Greeks spoke the same language and had the same religion, and they called everyone else 'barbarians' (because they joked that foreign languages sounded like 'bar-bar'). The Ancient Greeks thought they were special compared to barbarians and, annoyingly for the barbarians, in some ways they were!

TIME SLIME - TIME TO DRAIN YOUR BRAIN FOR A MINUTE

Ancient Greece happened a very, very long time ago. The years have oozed away. There are so many of them it gets confusing and our system of dating doesn't make things easier ...

Some of their wars weren't so midget. More on that later.

All years are dated before or after the supposed date of the birth of Christ, which happened during the time of the Roman Empire - after the Ancient Greeks had had their day. Years *after* the birth of Christ are called 'AD' which stands for the Latin *anno Domini*, meaning 'in the year of our Lord'. The AD years follow each other in a sensible fashion, thus AD 1999 comes after AD 1998 and so on.

Years before the birth of Christ are called 'BC' which stands for 'before Christ'. So the eighth century BC (800-700) is longer ago than the third century BC (300-200) and Alexander the Great for instance lived from 356-323 BC, which doesn't mean he lived backwards. In fact 'BC' ought to be called 'BTF' - 'Back To Front'!

THERE'S NO ESCAPE!

You may think that the Ancient Greeks are all over and done with. That they lived in the dim and distant past and that there's nothing left of them but a few crumbling temples and the odd statue or two.

How wrong you are. The Ancient Greeks are everywhere!

They're in the language you speak: in hundreds of words such as 'dinosaur' which means 'terrible lizard', or 'telephone' which comes from the Greek word *tele* meaning 'far' and *phone* meaning 'voice'.

 They're in the letters of our alphabet, which comes from the Greeks.

There's a bit of them in most buildings and a lot of paintings - the style of the Greeks is everywhere.

 Most of all they're in your brain! - if you believe that you have the right to think for yourself. It was the Ancient Greeks more than any other people who introduced science, democracy and freedom of speech.

Which is not to say that they were a bunch of freedom-loving artists who liked reading and writing. Before they got interested in freedom, they were a lot more interested in fighting ...

YOU'RE MY HERO!

WHERE WILD WARRIORS WANDER

ACHILLES' TENDON

Achilles was a hero. He was the greatest champion of the Greeks in their war with Troy , which probably ended around 1194 BC. The Trojan War was fought over Helen, the most beautiful woman in the world so they said.

According to legend, Achilles had a big advantage over other heroes: his body could not be wounded by weapons - all except one tender spot at the back of his heel  . If an enemy weapon struck him there, he was done for and, seeing as he was always fighting, it had to happen eventually. Achilles slaughtered lots and lots of Trojans but was finally killed by a poison arrow shot into his heel by a Trojan hero called Paris.

In modern Turkey.

This is why the big tendon which runs from the heel to the calf muscle is called the 'Achilles' tendon'.

The earliest Greeks that are known by name nowadays lived in the *Heroic Age* when times were tough and warfare was a way of life. In fact some people say that heroes like me and Achilles never existed at all! We may just be legends! Perish the thought... Later Greeks believed that us heroes were halfway between gods and men and made sacrifices to us. They knew how to treat a hero.

SEEK OUT THE GREEK PART I
(WOULD YOU MAKE A GOOD GREEK?)

Which of these heroic characteristics do you have?

(Answers on page 122)

Good at games

Brave

Loving to family and friends

Good looking

Ruthless and good at killing enemies

Crafty

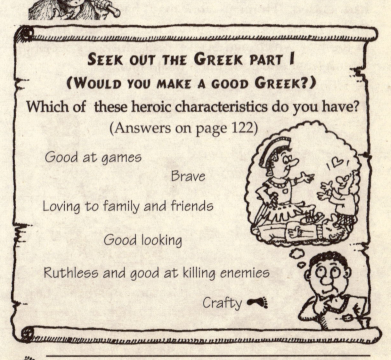

The early Greeks respected craftiness. In one story the goddess Athena comforts a hero called *Odysseus* with the words: 'Bold man, crafty in counsel, endlessly lying. Never, even in your own land, do you stop your cunning tricks and your lying stories which you love from the bottom of your heart'. She meant it as a compliment!

Blind bard

The story of the Trojan war where Achilles met his dreadful doom is told in *The Iliad*, the greatest of all Greek poems. *The Iliad* was more than a poem to the Ancient Greeks, it was the Bible and Shakespeare all rolled into one. They learned chunks of it at school and based plays and pictures on stories from it.

The Iliad and another long poem called *The Odyssey* were probably written by a poet called *Homer* in the 700s BC, several hundred years after the Trojan War had ended. Homer, who may have been blind, probably learned these stories from spoken accounts of the war which had been passed down by word of mouth from one generation to another.

The Iliad - the short version

There's a beauty contest between three goddesses. Paris (the Trojan hero who later killed Achilles) has given the prize (a golden apple) to the goddess Aphrodite 👣 .

In return Aphrodite helps Paris to kidnap Helen, the most beautiful woman in the world, from the Greeks.

Aphrodite (pronounced Afroditey) was goddess of love, beauty and fertility, among other things.

The Greeks get mad and attack the city of Troy in an attempt to get Helen back. For ten years they try to starve the people of Troy, but without success (although they have lots of adventures).

At last the Greeks hit on a cunning plan: they pretend to sail away, but they leave behind them a large, hollow wooden horse, with some soldiers hidden inside it.

The unsuspecting Trojans drag the horse into their city.

Late at night the hidden Greek soldiers climb out of the horse and open the gates of the city.

The rest of the Greek army, which has secretly sneaked back, then enters Troy, kills all the men, enslaves all the women and children and burns the city to the ground.

End of Troy and end of *The Iliad*.

Boy wonder

A hundred years ago most scholars thought that the stories of *The Iliad* and *The Odyssey* were just that - stories. Early Greece was a mystery and was over so long ago that no one expected to find out much about it.

Then along came an amazing man.

In AD 1830, when he was only eight, Heinrich Schliemann decided that he would spend his life looking for the lost city of Troy. At ten he wrote an essay in Latin about the Trojan War. At fourteen he became a cabin boy, was shipwrecked and survived. In his teens he went into business. During his travels as a business man he learned to speak English, French, Dutch, Spanish, Portuguese, Italian, Russian, Swedish, Polish and Arabic - as well as his native German. By the age of thirty-six he was rich enough to retire and follow his dream of searching for Troy - so he learned ancient and modern Greek as well!

Schliemann believed that *The Iliad* was a history book as well as a book of legends. From its description of Troy he decided that a hill in Turkey called Hissarlik was the most likely site of the ancient city. In 1870 he started digging. He, his wife and some Turkish workmen dug for a year and found nothing much except earth and rock. Then one day they uncovered a large copper bowl. It was crammed full with nine thousand objects made of gold and silver. Here was proof that Troy was more than a legend.

But he wasn't finished yet! As well as Troy, Schliemann wanted to prove that the Greek heroes were more than legends as well. He started digging in Greece at a place called *Mycenae* . Before long he

Mycenae is pronounced 'My-see-nee'.

had uncovered the remains of an ancient city where people had lived at the time of the Trojan war. Schliemann claimed that it was the town where Agamemnon, the Greek king in *The Iliad*, had lived, described by Homer as 'a well-built city, broad avenued and abounding in gold'.

AGE RAGE!

Schliemann wasn't right about everything he said about his discoveries, but almost alone he proved that a legendary civilization was real. Greece before the Trojan War is now called *Mycenaean* after his discovery in Greece and the time before the heroes is called the *Mycenaean Age*. The heroes themselves are called *Achaeans* 🦶 . The Achaeans may have conquered the Mycenaeans. No one knows for sure. Anyway their age is called the *Heroic Age* - with good reason!

Achaeans is pronounced 'Akeeyons'.

Gone with a Bang

The Mycenaeans learned their civilization from the island of Crete, where an even older civilization had grown up. Crete ruled the Mycenaeans for hundreds of years until about 1450 BC. It may be that Cretan power was ended by a massive volcanic eruption on the nearby island of Thera (the bit which still stands above the water is called Santorini) which would have sent huge tidal waves across the Mediterranean. Most of Thera disappeared in the explosion and many scholars think that Thera is the origin of the legend of the lost underwater civilization of *Atlantis*.

BOOM!

wow!

Larks in the Dark

The Mycenaeans and the Achaeans were warlike, but they weren't half as warlike as the Dorians who came after them. The Dorians came from the north around 1104 BC and fell on Greece like a pack of ravening wolves. These were the deepest dark ages of Greece. Civilization was almost totally destroyed, and the palaces and cities built up by the Mycenaeans crumbled into ruins.

FEELING MIFFED?

Greek myths part 1
Athens and the bull-headed monster

Athens was a major Mycenaean city but it was once subject to the Cretan Empire. It rose to power when a hero called Theseus, *son of a king of Athens back in the Mycenaean age, was sent to Crete as part of a yearly payment to the Cretan Empire of six youths and six maidens. The twelve youngsters were to be sacrificed to the* Minotaur, *a monster with the head of a bull and the body of a man. The Minotaur lived in a maze within the Cretan palace of Knossus. Greek legend said that Theseus killed the Minotaur, escaped from the maze and sailed back to Athens.*

When Theseus became king he is said to have united the villages around Athens under his rule, thus starting the polis of Attica *with Athens as its capital. When the Dorians invaded Greece many Mycenaeans (now called Ionians) fled to Athens, which was strong enough to protect them from Dorian attack.*

HELP! HOW DO WE FIND THE TOUR BUS WITHOUT THE MINOTAUR GETTING US??

CAN **YOU** DO THE AMAZING "**MINO-TOUR**" MAZE?

SNORT!

TOUR

The battered descendants of the Achaeans and the Ionians hung on to power in Attica and a few other places or

---

👣 *Aeolian* is pronounced 'Ee-oh-lian'. They were probably a mixture of Dorians and Ionians.

fled from the Dorians and started new colonies outside Greece.

RECIPE FOR ANCIENT GREECE

After the Dorian invasions were over, the clouds rolled back to reveal ancient Greek civilization as we know it today. The Ancient Greeks who created the golden, 'classical' age of Greece were a mixture of Dorians, Ionians and Aeolians.

They all thought of themselves as Greek because they spoke the same language - and worshipped the same gods.

GOAT-EARS MEETS BIRD-FACE

GODS, PEOPLE
- AND THINGS IN BETWEEN

STOP BEHAVING LIKE A GOD WILL YOU!

The gods of the Ancient Greeks came from a mixture of traditions, just like the people. A mixture of Mycenaean gods, such as Athena the goddess of Athens, and Dorian gods, such as Zeus the king of the gods. Often the two types of god married each other - although they didn't usually live happily ever after!

HERA AND ZEUS HAVING A TIFF

Greek gods behaved just like people except that they had god-like powers and could live for ever. They quarrelled, did stupid things, and fell in love and got married - although this never stopped them falling in love with someone else, including humans.

WELCOME TO THE GOD FAMILY AND THEIR FRIENDS AND RELATIONS

Ancient Greece was thick with gods. No wonder they argued so much: they had a god over-population problem! Most of the top gods were believed to be crowded on to the summit of Mount Olympus, a large mountain near the north east coast of Greece, but plenty of others lived underground or in the sea. In fact there were gods everywhere.

WHOOSH!!

POSEIDON - GOD OF THE SEA AND COASTLINES.

HERMES - MESSENGER OF THE GODS, AND GOD OF WORDS, CUNNING, BUSINESSMEN AND TRAVELLERS.

APHRODITE - GODDESS OF LOVE.

HI! APHIE!

PHOO!!

HI HADDIE! WHAT'S COOKING?

TO MOUNT OLYMPUS

HADES - GOD OF THE UNDERWORLD. ALSO CALLED PLUTO.

'MR. GOD' - ZEUS. TOP GOD. LOVES WOMEN, BOTH HUMAN AND GODDESSES. THROWS THUNDERBOLTS WHEN ANGRY.

'MRS. GOD' - HERA. WIFE OF ZEUS. QUEEN OF THE GODS. LOOKS AFTER WOMEN AND MARRIAGES. FROWNS ON ZEUS'S WILD BEHAVIOUR

APOLLO - GOD OF MUSIC AND THE SUN.

DIONYSUS - GOD OF WINE AND FUN. HIS FOLLOWERS WENT IN FOR DRUNKENNESS AND WILD BEHAVIOUR.

ARES - GOD OF WAR. HANDSOME AND BRAVE

DEMETER - GODDESS OF CORN.

ARTEMIS - GODDESS OF HUNTING.

ATHENA - GODDESS OF ATHENS. BRAVE AND BEAUTIFUL.

25

FEELING MIFFED?
Greek myths part 2
Oedipus and his mum and dad

When Oedipus 👣 *was born his feet were nailed to a mountain top because his father Laius had been told that his son would kill him. A shepherd saved Oedipus and brought him up.*

Later Oedipus was told by an oracle 🕊 *that he would kill his father and marry his mother. Oedipus took this to mean the shepherd and his wife, so he left home. Unfortunately he met his real father on the road (and didn't recognize him of course). The two men quarrelled and Oedipus killed his father.*

Later still Oedipus arrived in Thebes, where he saved the city from a dangerous monster called the Sphinx. His prize for doing this was to marry the queen Jocasta, but little did he know that Jocasta was his real mum. After they found out the truth Jocasta hanged herself and Oedipus blinded himself.

👣 *Oedipus* is pronounced 'Edepuss'.

👣 *Oracles* could see the future. See page 42.

THINGS IN BETWEEN

As if their country wasn't crowded enough with gods, the Ancient Greeks also believed in a whole host of creatures which weren't gods, but weren't real animals or humans either.

Question - what do you get if you marry a centaur with a harpy?
Answer - total confusion!

Centaurs were a wild herd, half horse and half human. They sometimes kidnapped women.

Harpies were a thoroughly bad lot. They were birds with women's faces which snatched things from people. Centaurs and harpies never did get married, but if they had, imagine what their babies might have looked like: horses with birds' heads, men with birds' bodies, women with horses' bodies. Take your pick!

Satyrs usually had horses' tails and goat ears, and they might have goat legs. They were lazy, cowardly and usually drunk.

Don't forget us heroes with our god-like powers. Usually we were the good guys and the Greeks held banquets in our honour. It wasn't just me and Achilles: there were heaps of heroes including the likes of Odysseus, Theseus - and Orpheus who went down to the Underworld to try to save his wife.

WHO'S TO BLAME?

Because the gods could behave badly, the Greeks didn't need a devil to explain the bad things that happen in the world. If someone was born clever or beautiful then obviously some god had been kind to them. On the other hand, if someone was born ugly or stupid then obviously he or she had been cursed by a god. The god didn't need to have had any particular reason - he or she might just have been feeling grumpy!

HUH! LOOK AT THAT STUPID HUMAN! WHISTLING! HE'S FAR TOO HAPPY! THIS WILL SORT HIM OUT!!

BAD LUCK SPELL

Gods were powerful, but you couldn't blame them for everything. The Ancient Greeks believed that happiness came to those people who made the right decisions in life (although they had to be lucky as well). That is, they believed that men and women were responsible for themselves. Here's how it works:

1. If you decide to work hard at school, you've got a better chance of ending up with a good job and lots of money than if you don't work hard.

2. Once you've got your well-paid job though, you may become proud and stuck up and think that you don't need gods to get on in life. This is what the Greeks called *hubris*. One thing is certain: if you suffer from hubris, the gods will punish you for it.

3. Of course it's always possible that you may get run over by a bus at any time! Well tough cheese, that's just the gods playing games and you can't do much about it - except try to keep the gods happy.

Well, it made sense to the Ancient Greeks!

SEEK OUT THE GREEK PART 2
Do you have godlike powers?
(Answers on page 122)

1. YOUR TEACHER HAS SPRUNG A SURPRISE TEST ON YOUR CLASS, BUT YOU HAVEN'T DONE ANY HOMEWORK. WHAT WILL YOU DO?..

a   Strike the teacher dead with a thunderbolt

b   Turn into a bull and gallop out of school

c   Grow little wings on your ankles and fly out of the classroom window

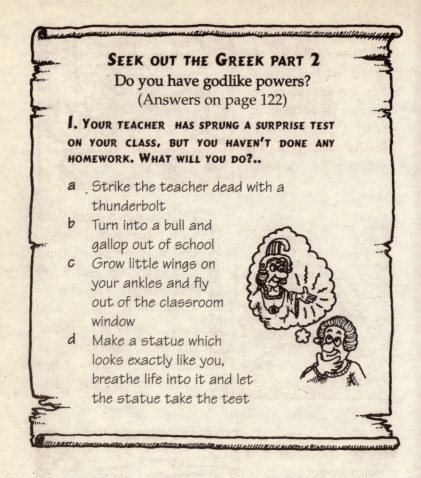

d   Make a statue which looks exactly like you, breathe life into it and let the statue take the test

TEMPLES IN THE SUN

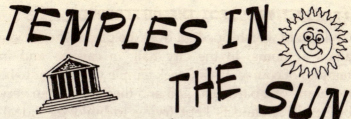

SLAP ON THE PAINT!

WHO'S FOR A SACRIFICE?

Ancient Greeks believed that gods liked the same things that humans like. To keep the gods happy the Greeks offered them everything that Greeks themselves enjoyed or found useful:

Achilles burnt humans on the funeral pyre of his friend Patroclus.

TEMPLE TIME - SPOT THE DIFFERENCE

Gods were worshipped all over the place. There were altars at home, in the city hall, in caves - and in temples of course. Each Greek temple was meant to be the home of a particular god and they were often very beautiful. Architects kept trying to build the 'ideal' temple - Greeks were very keen on ideals. The *ideal* version of something was the perfect version. It might never exist in reality, but at least they could try to imagine it. In their statues they tried to carve *ideal* people, on their pots they tried to paint *ideal* pictures.

Ancient Greek temples looked very different to the marble ruins which cling to the hills of modern Greece looking like worn out teeth today. They were brightly painted in reds, blues, yellows and greens, and they were shiny. Where the stone was left unpainted it might be stained with a mixture of saffron (a yellow spice) and milk. The whole thing would be covered in a sort of polish of wax and oil so as to stop the paint from fading and flaking in the hot sunshine.

THEN...

STATUE OF GOD OR GODDESS INSIDE THE TEMPLE

ALTAR

PRIEST

WELL-KEPT GARDEN

PARTHENON

The ruins of the *Parthenon*, the temple of Athena, still stand on a rocky hill above the modern city of Athens. The name means 'of the virgins' because it had a special room for Athena's virgin priestesses at the back. From the start in 447 BC the architects, Ictinus and Callicrates, meant it to be the ultimate in temple design.

It was perfectly built without any cement. The stone drums which make up the columns each had a hole at the ends big enough to fit a short round stick which thus connected two blocks together. During building the blocks were turned round and round against each other until they ground to a perfect fit. This was done to every block in every column.

Our eyes don't see things quite as they are. They play

THE VERTICAL COLUMNS SWELL IN THE CENTRE, THEN TAPER SLIGHTLY TO THE TOP. THIS TECHNIQUE IS CALLED **ENTASIS**. THE SAME TECHNIQUE IS USED ON HORIZONTAL PARTS OF BUILDINGS TO MAKE THEM LOOK STRAIGHTER!

tricks on us, making straight lines look slightly curved in places. The architects of the Parthenon were determined to make people see their temple the way it ought to be seen, so they made straight lines curve in the opposite direction to curves created by the naked eye - so as to make them seem straight!

DRESSED STONE

The gods had an over-population problem, but the population problem of the statues was far, far worse! Statues were a favourite and expensive offering to the gods. When Saint Paul visited Athens in the first century AD he found it a 'forest of idols', which was his way of saying it was full of statues. A special notice was carved in stone beside a temple in Rhodes forbidding anyone to leave any statues where they might obstruct the paths - the place was clogged up!

The statues were painted to look as realistic as possible, with special stones inlaid in the eyes for extra realism. This made them look very different to the blank stone remains which stare past us in museums today. It's as if the statues in the museums have died, which in a sense they have now that no one believes in them any more.

Statues of the gods were mainly kept inside the temples. Some of them were very old and badly carved and some were huge and beautifully carved. Either way they were treated with great care by the worshippers. They were washed and dressed in special clothes.

But sometimes statues had to watch out - if any disaster befell the worshippers the statue of the god or hero might be scolded for letting it happen. One later Greek empress had my statue whipped! She thought I'd been causing problems.

GIANT STATUES

The Colossus of Rhodes was the biggest statue by far but there were some other monsters.

The statue of Athena outside the Parthenon stood twenty-one metres high on its pedestal and on a clear day the sailors far out to sea could see the tip of her spear shining in the sun.

Inside the Parthenon was another vast statue of Athena, nearly twelve metres high (that's the height of a house). Her flesh was made of ivory and her robe was made of 1,154 kilograms of gold. This statue and an even larger one of Zeus at Olympus were made by a very famous Athenian sculptor called *Pheidias*.

His statue of Zeus at Olympia was *fourteen metres* high, also in ivory and gold. In front of it a shallow pool of olive oil kept the ivory moist and reflected light on to the statue. Special 'shiners' who claimed to be descended from the sculptor looked after the statue.

WILD WOMEN

In most religious ceremonies there would be a procession and the statue of the god (if it wasn't too large) might be carried through the streets. The procession wound its way to the altar in front of the god's temple where sacrifices were made.

That was a normal, tame ceremony, but the Greeks could do better when they chose. They had some really wild festivals. During the Festival of Dionysus, women known as *maenads* would dance and revel in the mountains and tear apart live animals to eat them raw.

SMELL SPELL

Some festivals were really spooky. It was said that the goddess Aphrodite once gave all the women of the island of Lemnos an evil smell so that their husbands rejected them. In memory of this, once a year for nine days all fires were extinguished, men and women were separated and all was grim and gloomy.

At the end of the nine days the fires were lit again and there was general relief and rejoicing.

SEEK OUT THE GREEK PART 3
Are you religious?

You have decided to ask Zeus to help you do well in a school test. But Zeus may get angry and scupper your chances if you don't do things right ...

(Answers on page 122)

I. WHICH OF THESE OFFERINGS MIGHT ZEUS APPRECIATE?

a   A pair of old trainers which make your room stink like a cheese factory

b   A computer game

c   Some chewed bubble gum

d   The flesh of your pet rabbit

e   A pizza

f   The family dog

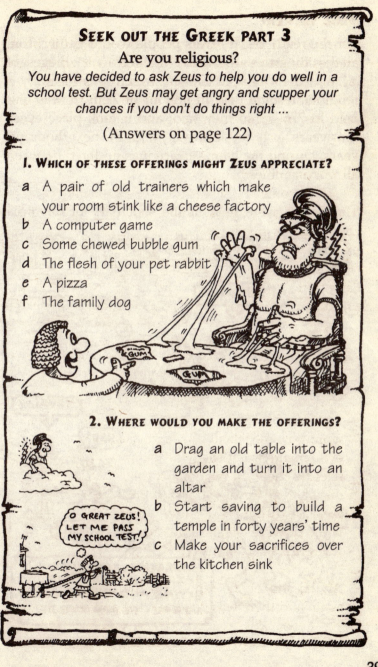

2. WHERE WOULD YOU MAKE THE OFFERINGS?

a   Drag an old table into the garden and turn it into an altar

b   Start saving to build a temple in forty years' time

c   Make your sacrifices over the kitchen sink

O GREAT ZEUS! LET ME PASS MY SCHOOL TEST!

TIME TO PLAY

For the really big festivals people would gather from all the city-states around the Mediterranean. Biggest of all was the Olympic Games, which was basically a religious festival held in honour of Zeus. It was first held in 776 BC, so they said, and it took place every four years (as it does nowadays) for the next thousand years. During the games peace was declared between all warring cities.

The games were held at the sanctuary of Olympia

where there was space for forty-five thousand spectators. Only men were allowed in and huge crowds of them would camp there during the festival. Athletes competed naked. Once a woman slipped in disguised as a trainer. She gave herself away by leaping over the barrier when her son won a prize, and she was only spared death because she was the mother of a champion.

From then on the trainers had to go naked when they came to be registered as well as the athletes.

Do as I say, not as I do

High up on Mount Parnassus there are deep gorges where horrid gases escape from the Earth. The Ancient Greeks called this place the 'Navel of the World'. Around it they built the temples and altars of the sacred city of Delphi.

They used to visit Delphi to question the *oracle* in the temple of Apollo. An oracle was a bit like a prophetess. One of three priestesses, the *Pythia*, would perch on a high tripod over a deep cleft in the floor of the temple. Breathing deeply of the gases which rose from the cleft she would fall into a drugged trance. In this state she was ready to answer questions, which she did in a mumble of drugged gobbledegook. Priests

---

Navel means 'tummy button'.

standing by would translate the gobbledegook for the questioner. On the whole they advised people to be moderate and to make peace rather than war.

Which was a good thing because the city states were always arguing with each other.

POLIS! POLIS!

HERAKLES OUT!

THE STATE OF THE CITIES

A CROP OF POLIS

Each early Greek city-state grew from a few farms and pirate villages built within easy reach of a central fortress or *acropolis* where people could run for safety if attacked. Times were tough in the Heroic Age and they took no chances: the *Acrocorinthus* at Corinth is perched on a hill six hundred metres high and watered by a spring which never runs dry. The Acropolis of Athens, where the Parthenon stands, is a high, rocky outcrop protected by cliffs. Gradually temples, markets and other buildings grew up around these fortresses, nestling close up like ducklings beneath the

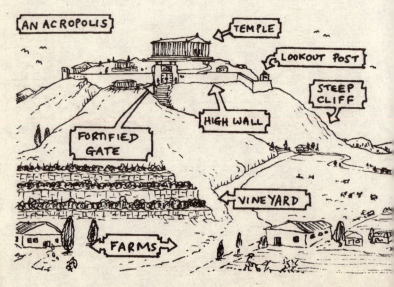

AN ACROPOLIS

TEMPLE

LOOKOUT POST

STEEP CLIFF

HIGH WALL

FORTIFIED GATE

VINEYARD

FARMS

wing of a mother duck. The citizens ruled themselves because there were no big empires near enough to boss them around. Independence and freedom were very important to your average Ancient Greek.

GRADES ON THE GOVERNOMETER

Every polis had its own way of doing things. Greece was like an experimental laboratory for types of government.

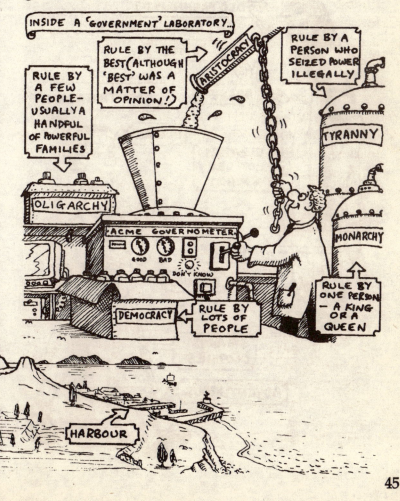

Athens v. Sparta

Of all the different polis with their different styles of government, two became specially powerful. These two had very different governments and they produced different sorts of citizens.

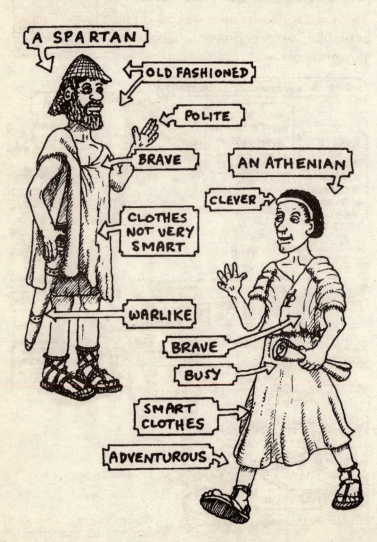

A SPARTAN

OLD FASHIONED

POLITE

BRAVE

CLOTHES NOT VERY SMART

WARLIKE

AN ATHENIAN

CLEVER

BRAVE

BUSY

SMART CLOTHES

ADVENTUROUS

DEMOCRACY. HOW IT ALL BEGAN

Athens was where democracy first flowered.

The Greeks understood that if they were to live freely they had to have laws which everyone agreed to, otherwise they might as well go and live in the forest and scamper about with the wild centaurs.

The very first Greek laws to be written down were in Locria, a colony in Italy, not in Athens. These laws were so popular that the Locrians didn't want to change or add to them. If anyone wanted to propose a new law in Locria he had to speak with a rope round his neck - so that he could be hung quickly if his new law was voted down!

In 621 BC *Draco* wrote down the laws of Athens. The laws were so tough that even today we call a tough law 'draconian'.

In 594 BC the Athenians asked a poet called *Solon* to sort out their laws and their system of government. He decided that from now on even the poorest citizen should have a vote in the 'Assembly' where the laws were made. Solon's laws were wiser and kinder than Draco's.

In 507 BC, along came *Cleisthenes*, the ultimate democrat. He enlarged the Assembly so that there were thirty thousand members.

Pericles was top man in Athens from about 450-30 BC. This period was the golden age of Athenian democracy. He arranged for wages to be paid to all who held public offices, such as magistrates. This meant that even poor men could have some power because they could afford to stop work while they were in office.

POTTERY LOTTERY

Cleisthenes invented *ostracism*. This was a way of getting rid of anyone who had grown too powerful. On the day of an ostracism each citizen wrote the name of someone he wanted to get rid of on an old bit of pot, called an *ostrakon*. When all the bits of pot were counted (as long as more than six thousand citizens had voted), whoever got their name written down the most was banished from Athens for ten years.

Actually only ten people were ever ostracised - and one of these may have been Cleisthenes himself!

Pnyx tricks

Day-to-day business in Athens was run by a small group of randomly chosen officials called the *boule*. But really important decisions were taken by the Assembly. The Athenian Assembly met on a hill called the *Pnyx* close to the Acropolis and all citizens had the right to attend its meetings.

As well as voting at the Assembly or being chosen for official positions, citizens over thirty years old could serve on juries at the law courts. Some courts had huge juries of 1001 men, although most had 501. The time allowed for speeches at the law courts was strictly controlled: small crimes meant short speeches. The worse the crime and the possible punishment, the longer the speeches which were allowed to be made.

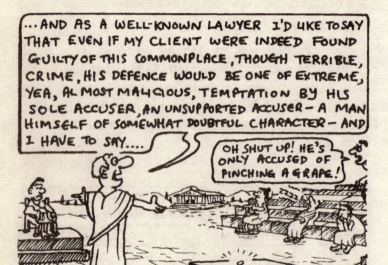

SLAVE GRADES

Athenian democracy wasn't quite like modern democracy. Only citizens could vote, which meant that slaves , foreigners and women couldn't - because they weren't citizens! It sounds unfair, but all ancient states had slaves and it was only in Greece that anyone could vote at all.

Greek thinkers called *cynics* and *stoics* disapproved of slavery. More on them later.

Everyone wanted to own a slave; they were expensive but useful, like owning a car nowadays. Athenians were kinder to their slaves than most people: unlike in most other states, they weren't allowed to kill them.

Slaves wore the same clothes as ordinary Athenians so no one could see that they were slaves when they were out and about, and their masters would often hire

them out to work for wages. They earned the same as free workmen - but their masters kept five-sixths of the wages! They could save up the rest to buy their freedom.

The luckiest slaves were the flute girls who were hired out to entertain at parties, and the skilled workmen. Both could earn quite large sums of money.

Athenian kindness didn't stretch as far as the law courts (by law slaves had to be tortured before giving evidence), or the silver mines of Laurium. The slaves

who worked in the silver mines were really unlucky. Owners made so much money that they could afford to buy a new slave every three years with money made from the old one. The miners lived up to ninety metres underground. They had to crawl or kneel at their work. Air was fed to them down narrow shafts where fires were burned halfway down to create a draft.

HEAD SLAVE

In the sixth century BC a slave called Drimachus led a slave revolt on the island of Chios where there was a big slave market. He defeated all armies led against him. From his mountain stronghold he took money from rich citizens and forced them to be kinder to their slaves. Finally he had his head chopped off so that his friends could claim the reward offered for it.

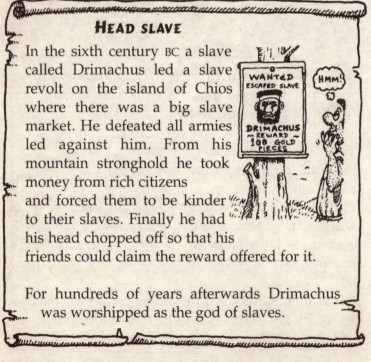

For hundreds of years afterwards Drimachus was worshipped as the god of slaves.

ARE YOU STUPID?

See how many of these questions you can answer and find out.

1. WHAT DID MAENADS DO?

a Refuse to lend things to people
b Revel in the mountains
c Live separately from men for nine days

2. WHAT IS A HARPY?

a A harpist
b Someone who drinks too much lager
c A bird with a woman's face

3. WHO WROTE THE ILIAD?

a Homer
b Agamemnon
c Troy

Answers 1 - b, 2 - c, 3 - a. Three right - you're okay, two right - you're still okay, none right - go and talk to a plank if you need company.

53

Secret Spartans

Athens was free and easy. It welcomed foreigners and many foreign craftsmen lived there.

Sparta was very different. If any foreigner stayed too long in Sparta the police would march them to the frontier. In Sparta there were seven slaves (called *helots*) to each free citizen. The Spartans were Dorians and the helots were the remains of the people they had conquered during the Dorian invasion around 1,100 BC. Helots were owned by the state and a secret police force kept them in line. Once a year for a day the Spartans declared war on their helots. On that day they could kill them on sight.

And tough Spartans

Spartans were tough - very tough.

1. The toughness started at birth. Every new born baby was brought before a state committee. If it was judged faulty or defective it was thrown from a cliff! Also fathers had the right to kill their new born children, if they thought they weren't up to scratch in some way.

See page 19.

2. At the age of seven every Spartan boy went to live in an army barracks. He had no more home life until he was in his thirties.

3. The boys had to sleep out of doors every night winter and summer.

4. Boys were allowed only one piece of clothing per year, and they didn't bathe very often.

5. Older men encouraged the boys to quarrel and fight so as to encourage a warlike attitude.

No wonder the Spartans were the best soldiers in Ancient Greece. In all of Sparta there was just one temple to Aphrodite the goddess of love. Her statue carried a sword and was chained at the feet to show that war was more important than love.

AND SHOUTING SPARTANS

The Spartan laws were said to have been written by a one-eyed leader called *Lycurgus*. His other eye was struck out by an opponent. After he had written his laws he retired to Delphi and starved himself to death.

Spartans were old-fashioned and very careful when it came to governing themselves. They had a monarchy (with two kings, just to be on the safe side). The kings commanded the army in war.

They also had a senate, or *gerousia*. 'Gerousia' meant a group of old men, and this is exactly what it was. Those under sixty were thought to be too young to govern the country. Candidates for the gerousia were chosen by shouting. The old men had to walk silently before the assembly of citizens, which met once a month on the day of the full moon. Those who got the longest and loudest shouts was declared chosen!

Spartans, in spite of living in barracks and being commanded by kings and old men, thought of themselves as free men like the rest of the Greeks. They called themselves *homoioi*, which meant 'equals'.

Of course only citizens could be equals. As in Athens, that ruled out slaves, foreigners and women - although Spartans had a problem with their women ...

HOMES, COMBS AND POEMS

HER INDOORS - AND NOT INDOORS

SPIRITED SPARTANS

Women were never treated as equals by men in the Ancient World, but some were a lot more equal than others. Above all, Spartan women were famous for their free and easy ways. They could speak their minds and boss their husbands. Girls took part in many games with each other such as running and wrestling. And they exercised naked like the men, which shocked Greeks from other cities.

It's hard not to feel sorry for the poor old Spartan men sleeping out of doors or dining in their barracks while their women were living it up at home. The women could inherit land and, since the men kept being killed in wars, by the third century BC a fifth of all the land in Sparta belonged to women. Which seemed like a lot to the Ancient Greeks.

SEEK OUT THE GREEK PART 4

Are you beautiful?

There was no plastic surgery in Ancient Greece, but if an Ancient Greek man had been able to visit a plastic surgeon, which of the following might he have chosen in order to match the Greek ideal of beauty?

(Answers on page 122)

I. A CHOICE OF NOSES

a   A nose which runs in a straight line from the forehead

b   A snub nose

c   A huge, hooked, hairy nose

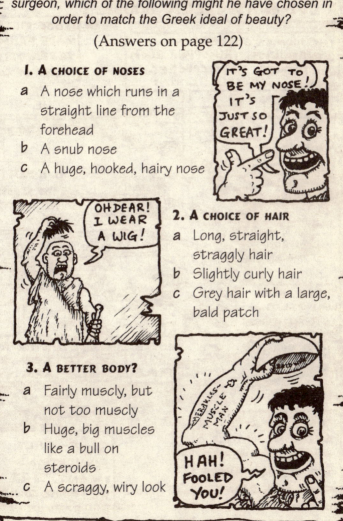

IT'S GOT TO BE MY NOSE! IT'S JUST SO GREAT!

OH DEAR! I WEAR A WIG!

2. A CHOICE OF HAIR

a   Long, straight, straggly hair

b   Slightly curly hair

c   Grey hair with a large, bald patch

3. A BETTER BODY?

a   Fairly muscly, but not too muscly

b   Huge, big muscles like a bull on steroids

c   A scraggy, wiry look

MUSCLE MAN

HAH! FOOLED YOU!

Unlucky Athenians

Athenian women weren't so lucky. They spent most of their lives at home and lived their lives separately from the men. If a woman went out she probably wore a veil.

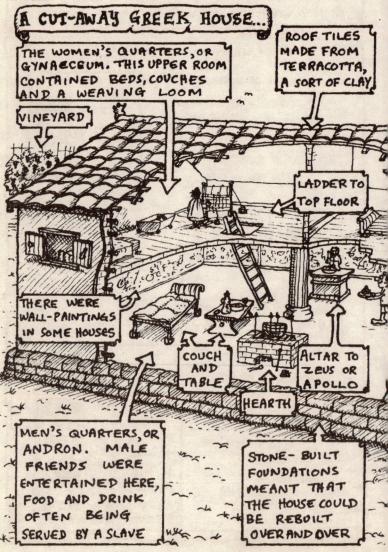

A CUT-AWAY GREEK HOUSE...

THE WOMEN'S QUARTERS, OR GYNAECEUM. THIS UPPER ROOM CONTAINED BEDS, COUCHES AND A WEAVING LOOM

ROOF TILES MADE FROM TERRACOTTA, A SORT OF CLAY

VINEYARD

LADDER TO TOP FLOOR

THERE WERE WALL-PAINTINGS IN SOME HOUSES

COUCH AND TABLE

ALTAR TO ZEUS OR APOLLO

HEARTH

MEN'S QUARTERS, OR ANDRON. MALE FRIENDS WERE ENTERTAINED HERE, FOOD AND DRINK OFTEN BEING SERVED BY A SLAVE

STONE-BUILT FOUNDATIONS MEANT THAT THE HOUSE COULD BE REBUILT OVER AND OVER

Athenian houses were divided into women's quarters and men's quarters. Women spent their days in the loom room, working and talking with friends and family. Fleeces were brought 'straight from the sheep' and all the spinning and weaving was done there. They also ground the flour for bread and baked it.

ROOF-ENDS WERE SOMETIMES DECORATED WITH HUMAN OR ANIMAL FACES

WEALTHY HOUSEHOLDS MAY HAVE HAD A BATHROOM

OLIVE GROVE

SHUTTERED WINDOWS (NO GLASS)

STORAGE CELLAR

HOUSES WERE WOOD-FRAMED, WITH MUD BRICKS AND PLASTER

PORCH PILLARS (USUALLY WOODEN)

HERMS STOOD BEFORE MANY HOUSES TO PROTECT THEM FROM EVIL SPIRITS. THESE WERE ORIGINALLY STATUES OF HERMES, WHO WAS A ROADSIDE DEMON BEFORE BECOMING THE MESSENGER OF THE GODS.

SAPPHO'S STORY

Sappho was born on the island of Lesbos around 630 BC. She was perhaps the greatest of all the Greek poets, and she was a woman. When she was young she used to speak her mind and got involved in politics. Around 600 BC she was banished to Sicily where she married a rich merchant and had a little daughter. After her husband died she returned to Lesbos and opened a school for women. There she taught, made friends and wrote love poems to several of her pupils.

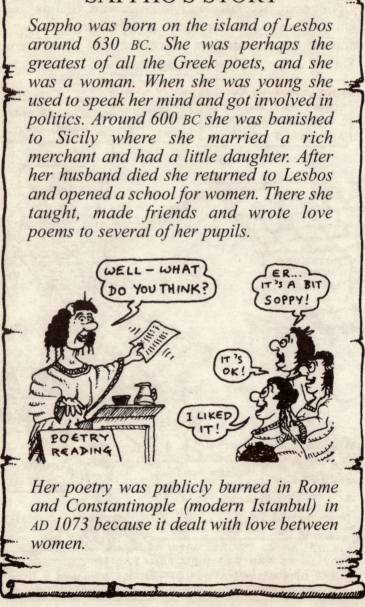

Her poetry was publicly burned in Rome and Constantinople (modern Istanbul) in AD 1073 because it dealt with love between women.

Feeling companiable?

Sappho called her pupils *hetairai*, meaning companions. 'Hetaira' was the name later given by the Athenians to certain free women who lived in their city. They were often very clever and beautiful. A special law made them wear flowery robes and they were forbidden to enter temples.

The most famous of them was *Aspasia*, the lover of the law-giver Perikles. Perikles and Aspasia lived together as man and wife although they never married. It was forbidden for an Athenian like Pericles to marry a foreigner like Aspasia. Aspasia was independently minded like many hetairai. She opened a famous school in Athens where women were welcome.

HAIR CARE AND OTHER PROBLEMS

Aspasia had blond hair. The Greeks liked blonds and since most of them are dark there were many, men included, who dyed their hair, especially hetairai.

Greek women also dolloped on the make-up.

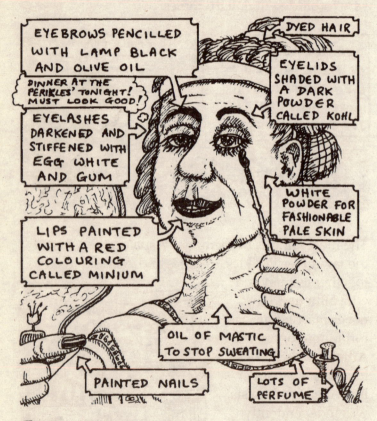

EYEBROWS PENCILLED WITH LAMP BLACK AND OLIVE OIL

DINNER AT THE PERIKLES' TONIGHT! MUST LOOK GOOD!

EYELASHES DARKENED AND STIFFENED WITH EGG WHITE AND GUM

LIPS PAINTED WITH A RED COLOURING CALLED MINIUM

DYED HAIR

EYELIDS SHADED WITH A DARK POWDER CALLED KOHL

WHITE POWDER FOR FASHIONABLE PALE SKIN

OIL OF MASTIC TO STOP SWEATING

PAINTED NAILS

LOTS OF PERFUME

FASHION PARADE

Both sexes wore a simple linen garment next to the skin. By the sixth century BC a lighter linen garment, called a *chiton* began to be worn. A cloak called a *himation* was worn in cold weather or for travelling.

Women tended to wear bright colours, although for a time it was illegal for poor people to wear red chitons in public. Women took a great interest in their dress, and they might wear padding to make their figures look better.

FANCY HAIR-DO, WITH RIBBONS AND A HAIR NET

LONG HAIR AND BEARD. AFTER ABOUT 490 BC, GREEKS CUT THEIR HAIR SHORTER

HATS WERE UNPOPULAR. IT WAS THOUGHT THAT THEY MADE THE HAIR GO GREY EARLY

THE CLOAK WAS USED TO COVER THE HEAD WHEN IN PUBLIC

ARE YOU READY YET? I'M STARVING!

I'VE GOT NOTHING TO WEAR!

PINS

PINS

MEN WORE AT LEAST ONE RING

CLOAK, CALLED A HIMATION

SOME WOMEN WORE A BRA MADE OF A STRIP OF LINEN

A CHITON. MEN SOMETIMES TUCKED THESE IN A BELT TO MAKE THEM SHORTER, OR WORE A SHORT CLOAK CALLED A CHLAMYS

MEN DIDN'T WEAR UNDERWEAR

FASHIONABLE SHOES. LOW, PURPLE ONES WERE POPULAR WITH THE WOMEN OF THEBES

MOST PEOPLE WORE SANDALS OUTDOORS

The women's love of good clothes must have caused problems; an Athenian law forbade women to take more than three dresses when travelling.

GET MARRIED OR ELSE!

Most Greeks got married. But in Sparta it was a crime to stay single. Spartan bachelors were made to march naked even in winter singing a special song about how they deserved such treatment. If they kept on refusing to marry they might be attacked in the streets by gangs of women. Groups of men who still wouldn't get married were shoved in a dark room with an equal number of women and had to choose their mates in total darkness!

Ancient Greek marriages were usually arranged by the parents and took place at fifteen years old for girls and thirty for men. Before the wedding the girl gave her toys to a temple as a sign that she was putting her childhood behind her. When the day came for the wedding, both bride and

SOME GREEK TOYS...

WHIP AND TOP

KNUCKLEBONE JACKS

CLAY DOLL

MARBLES

groom took special baths and the bride put on her white wedding robes and veil.

The high point was a big marriage feast where men and women sat separately. Feasting and wine-drinking were two things the Ancient Greeks were very good at.

A MAN'S GOTTA DO WHAT A MAN'S GOTTA DO

HARD-WORKING SHOPPER SEEKS DINNER AFTER THEATRE

SICKPOSIUM

Everyone drank lots of wine, even small children. It was always mixed - three parts of water to two parts wine, but that didn't stop adults getting drunk. The men often drank too much at *symposiums*, or men's dinner parties.

All except the Spartans - who had to be different of course. They had a special way of teaching their young men the dangers of drunkenness: a slave would be made to drink as much as possible in front of the young men so that they could see how stupid he became!

ARE YOU INCREDIBLY CLEVER?

Some of the cleverest people who have ever lived were Ancient Greeks. One of these was Zeno of Elea (c.430-490 BC.) Can you make sense of Zeno's paradoxes?

1. Achilles is chasing a tortoise. Why can he never catch it?

FINISH

2. Why can a runner never finish his race?

3. Why is an arrow fired from a bow motionless in mid-air?

Answers

1. Whenever Achilles reaches the point where the tortoise ought to be, the tortoise will have moved on, because the tortoise is always moving.

2. A runner must run the first half of his race before the second, and then the third quarter before the fourth - he will forever halve the distance to the finishing post and then halve the half and so on - and so will never reach it.

3. An arrow can be at only one point in space at any one moment. While it's there it must be motionless because it can't be in one place and be moving at the same time.

AND SINGPOSIUM

Symposiums were held in the *andron,* or men's room. The men lay on couches with a small table beside each couch. When the family ate together women sat on stools and children might have to sit on the floor. Diners at a symposium wore garlands of flowers on their heads and ate and talked for hours on end. Flute

A SYMPOSIUM...

WREATHS WERE HUNG ON WALLS

STREAMERS OF IVY OR VINE LEAVES

SOMETIMES TEXTILE DRAPERIES WERE HUNG OVER DOORS AND WINDOWS

FLUTE GIRLS

HAH! HAH! LET'S PLAY 'SPLASH THE SLAVE'!

STAND STILL!

SPLASH!

HOO! GOOD SHOT!

Wine cups had strong handles so that they could be used to play a game called *kottabos*. This meant flicking the dregs of wine at a target. In one version the aim was to sink small saucers floating in a bowl.

I SAY YOU CHAPS! THAT'S JUST NOT CRICKET!

girls could be hired for the evening and the diners would sing or recite poetry while the girls accompanied them. Flute girls were usually foreign and young Athenian men often fell in love with them. Eventually marriages with foreigners had to be allowed because so many men were living with foreign women anyway.

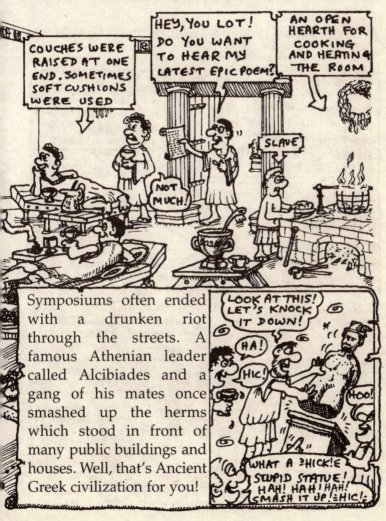

Symposiums often ended with a drunken riot through the streets. A famous Athenian leader called Alcibiades and a gang of his mates once smashed up the herms which stood in front of many public buildings and houses. Well, that's Ancient Greek civilization for you!

Shop till you drop!

Men didn't spend much time indoors except in the evenings. They had to work and in Athens they had to do the shopping as well because the women couldn't go out much. Mostly the men shopped at the *agora*, which was a central space in the middle of the city surrounded by shops and public buildings.

A hard day's shopping (well, a very hard day's shopping) might include:

OR WORK TILL YOU SHOP

Most free citizens had to work for their living . Those who weren't farmers had to start learning a trade when they were fifteen. The wage for a humble building worker was a drachma a day, which was enough to feed a family for a week. Craftsmen earned more.

Some, such as the potters and sculptors, were highly skilled artists. Typically for Ancient Greeks, they were always trying out new designs. Fashions in pots changed so rapidly that it's possible to date Athenian history to within ten years just by looking at the remains of pots from a particular period.

AN AMPHORA (STORAGE JAR)
- RED FIGURES ON A BLACK BACKGROUND
[c. 530 BC]

A SKYTHOS (WINE BOWL)
- BLACK FIGURES ON A RED BACKGROUND
[c. 540 BC]

Except in places such as Sparta and Syracuse in Sicily where there were lots of slaves.

DAYS OF PLAYS

It's a good thing the climate is so warm and mild in Greece. Men would often spend all day outside and not come home till late at night. Even entertainment happened outdoors. Theatre, which the Ancient Greeks pretty well invented, took place in massive outdoor arenas. The big one at Athens could seat fifteen thousand. Everyone, including women, went along. The state even paid the entrance fees of poor citizens.

The height of the theatre season was the festival of Dionysus, god of wine and madness, called the 'Great Dionysia', when there were three days of plays - at five plays per day! It seems that most people sat through all five plays, although the clever ones brought cushions. The statue of Dionysus was brought to the theatre so that he could enjoy the show as well. Each day there were three new *tragedies* which were sad serious plays, one new *comedy* and a *satyr play*, a comedy where the chorus dressed as satyrs with goat legs and ears. The day before the theatre there was a wild opening party when as many as 240 bulls might be sacrificed and eaten, and lakes of wine were drunk. At the end of the festival prizes were given to the writers of the best plays.

POET PORTRAITS

In the years 550-350 the Ancient Greeks produced a glorious gallery of brilliant writers. Here are a few of the most famous:

Aeschylus 525-456 BC. A soldier who fought at the famous Battle of Marathon. The first great writer of tragedies, he won the Great Dionysia thirteen times until he was beaten by *Sophocles* in 468. Then he went off to live in Sicily. He is said to have died when an eagle dropped a tortoise on his head.

75

Sophocles 496-406/5 BC. Wrote 130 tragedies and won the Great Dionysia eighteen times. His most famous play *Oedipus Tyrannus* is about a king  who unknowingly marries his mother.

Euripides 485-406 BC. Wrote violent tragedies. His most famous play *Electra* is about the revenge of King Agamemnon's son and daughter on their mother. Said to have been killed by the dogs of the King of Macedon.

Aristophanes 445-385 BC. He was the king of comedy. His most famous play *Lysistrata* is about a quarrel between men and women.

LAST MOVEMENT

Writers wrote the music which went with their plays. Music was everywhere in Ancient Greece: at the theatre, at dinner parties, even when they went to war.

The Spartans as usual did it their own way. They had

See page 26.

a law which punished anyone who did not play music in the 'Doric' or Spartan style. Their most famous musician *Terpander* 'Delighter of Men' had his harp nailed to the wall because he dared to add an extra string!

Terpander died at a dinner party. One of his audience threw a fig at him while he was singing. It went straight in his open mouth, stuck in his throat and choked him.

FOOLS AND SCHOOLS

IT'S THE NAKED TRUTH

All Greek citizens were expected to be able to read and write. But first of all they needed an alphabet.

ALPHABET SOUP

OLD GREEK	CLASSICAL GREEK	ROMAN
Δ	A	A
8	B	B
∧	Γ	C
Δ	Δ	D
∃	E	E
∃	Φ	F
		G
日	H	H
I	I	I
		J
メ	K	K
∧	∧	L
M	M	M
Ч	N	N
O	O	O
┑	π	P
Φ		Q
۹	P	R
Ч	Σ	S
Ɣ	T	T
Υ	Υ	U
		V
		W
X	Ξ	X
I	Z	Y
		Z

Our word 'alphabet' comes from the first two letters of the Greek alphabet: *alpha* (Δ) and *beta* (8). The Greeks learned to write from the *Phoenicians* around the fourteenth century BC. To start with they wrote from right to left, then they wrote both ways 'like ploughing a field' and they ended up writing from left to right as we do. Later the Romans copied one of their writing styles and this is where our modern 'Roman' alphabet comes from. Thank you, Ancient Greeks, or, as they would have written it:

ΕΥΦΗΑΡΙΣΤΟ!

👣 The Phoenicians lived on the coast of what is now the Lebanon, just across the Mediterranean.

Boys' world

Boys went to school from six until up to sixteen. If they were rich they walked there with their *paidagogos*, a slave whose job was to make sure they worked hard and to beat them if they misbehaved. There were no desks, just benches. Pupils learned music, writing (which included reading and arithmetic) and gymnastics.

For gymnastics the teacher had a choice of two places to take his pupils.

1. The local *palaestra* or wrestling school
2. The local *gymnasium*

There were three gymnasiums in Athens, all outside the city walls: the *Academy*, the *Lyceum* and the *Cynosarges*. Gymnasiums got their name because of the Greek habit of exercising naked - the word means 'place where people go naked'. A typical gymnasium would have dressing and washing rooms, a running track, sandy areas for boxing and perhaps a kind of swimming bath.

Gymnasiums were great places for meeting people. The men did a lot of sitting around and talking between exercises. Because of all the talking and arguing that went on they became places to exercise the mind as well as the body. Many later ones even had lecture halls and libraries and turned into something like universities. The first gymnasium to develop in this way was the *Academy*, where a 'school' for young men was started in 388 BC. Shortly after, another school was started at the *Lyceum*.

SCHOOLS FOR THOUGHT

There are ordinary schools for teaching children, and there are schools of *philosophy*. Greeks produced schools of philosophy like hens lay eggs. In Ancient Greek a *philosopher* meant a lover of *sophos,* or wisdom. We still use the same word today for someone who thinks deeply about the problems of life, death and the universe.

*Pythagoras c.*582-*c.*497 BC was a brilliant mathematician who wore long white trousers and a golden crown so as to attract attention to himself. Both women and men could join his school. He was vegetarian and believed that animals and people have souls which can be reborn again and again. His followers tried not to hurt anyone, not even slaves.

*Zeno of Citium c.*333-262 BC had a weak head which hung to one side, but a strong brain. His school 'the stoics' got its name from the *Stoa Poecile* or painted porch in Athens where he used to teach. He believed in living quietly and suggested that hunger was the best cure for love.

*Diogenes c.*400-325 BC was a bankrupt banker who dressed like a beggar and claimed that the secret of happiness is to live very simply. He envied the life of animals and tried to copy it, living in a tub like a kennel. He belonged to the school of the *cynics*, from the Greek word for a dog . He is said to have killed himself by holding his breath .

The school of the *cynics* was founded at the Cynosarges gymnasium in Athens. *Cynos-arges* means 'dog-fish'.

This is probably impossible because each time he went unconscious he would have started breathing again.

Plato c.428-348 BC was a muscular Athenian aristocrat who got his nickname *Platon* meaning 'broad' because he was good at wrestling. He loved the Spartan way of doing things and scorned democracy. Platonists argue (among other things) that behind the world we live in lies an 'ideal' world, and that the world we live in is like a shadow of the ideal world. It was Plato who started the school at the Academy. Women were allowed to join.

Aristotle 384-322 BC was one of Plato's pupils. He was interested in everything from types of plants to types of government. In some ways he was more like a modern scientist than a philosopher. He started the school at the Lyceum.

FEELING MIFFED?

Greek myths part 3
Icarus flies too high

Daedalus was an inventor and a craftsman. His sculptures were so lifelike that they stood up and walked away unless they were chained to their pedestals. Unfortunately he angered the king of Minos, where he was staying, and Minos shut him and his son Icarus up in the maze where the Minotaur had been kept.

Daedalus made wings for them both. They flew over the palace walls and out over the Mediterranean Sea. Daedalus warned his son not to fly too close to the Sun, but Icarus ignored him. He flew higher and higher until the heat of the Sun melted the wax on his wings and he fell to Earth.

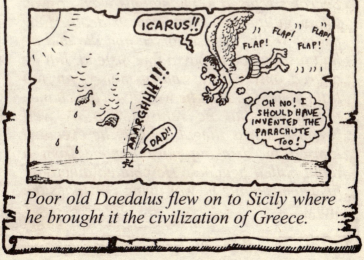

Poor old Daedalus flew on to Sicily where he brought it the civilization of Greece.

THE STUBBORN STORY
OF SOCRATES

Socrates (c.470-399 BC) was a war hero. He was short, fat and ugly and good at talking. He used to teach his pupils, including Plato, by asking them questions so that they had to think hard about what they said.

The Athenians got fed up with the way he taught their sons to question the gods and democracy. He was brought to trial and sentenced to death for 'introducing new gods and corrupting the young'. (All right, freedom of speech wasn't perfect, even in Ancient Athens.)

Socrates refused to change his ways so was found guilty and sentenced to death. Few people really wanted to see him die and he had the chance to pay a fine instead. But he offered only a tiny sum of money, far too little to get off. Next he was given the chance to escape, but he refused that as well because it was illegal. Finally he executed himself by drinking poison made from a plant called hemlock. He chatted quietly to his friends while he was dying - or that's the story.

A GALAXY OF GREATS

Greek philosophers came up with some very modern ideas - and some which seem plain crazy. Already by 400 BC some of them had worked out that the Earth was round and that the Moon shone by reflected light.

Thales 625-547 BC was the first of the famous Greek philosophers. He thought everything in the world must be made of water. Wrong, Thales! But full marks for trying.

Anaximander c.610-546 BC decided that the Earth must be curved and claimed that land animals evolved from fish. Nine out of ten, Anaximander.

Anaxagoras c.500-c.428 BC said that everything could be divided into smaller and smaller pieces for ever. He said the Sun was huge and hot and there must be other worlds with life on them. Ten out of ten - probably!

Democritus c.470-c.380 BC decided that everything was made up of tiny particles or 'atoms'. Ten out of ten.

A CRAZY IDEA.

Xenophanes c.570-478 BC argued that the Earth must be flat because that's how it looks. So the Sun doesn't set; it just disappears into the distance and a brand new Sun appears in the morning. Zero marks for accuracy, but a couple for trying!

Democritus decided when he wanted to die. Having lived long enough he reduced his food daily and gradually starved himself. He stayed alive three days longer than he had originally intended so that he could watch a festival. During those three days he kept himself going by holding hot loaves to his nostrils.

THE BITTER TRUTH

You might think that an age when people did so much quiet thinking must have been an age of peace and plenty, but that's only half the truth. The golden age of the philosophers was never very peaceful. Take Miletus, on the coast of modern Turkey, which was where the very first philosophers such as Thales and Anaximander came from. In the fifth century the poor of Miletus kicked out the rich and set oxen on their remaining children, trampling them to death. The rich then returned, coated the leaders of the democracy with tar and burned them alive.

Likewise the death of Socrates was not nearly as peaceful as described by his pupil Plato. Plato writes that Socrates died while talking quietly to his friends after he had drunk the hemlock with which he executed himself. But nothing could have been further from the truth.

To start with, his trial came after a long period of civil war when the people of Athens had suffered plague, starvation and tyranny. And real hemlock is a bitter drug which causes choking and uncontrollable shaking before it kills.

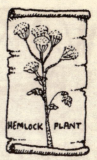

But then Socrates was tough, like most of the Ancient Greeks. In one battle against the Spartans he had been the last Athenian to retreat and saved himself by glaring so fiercely at the enemy that they held back!

Like most Greeks he was a soldier first and a philosopher, artist, politician or whatever else second.

WAR AND GORE

LET'S SOLDIER ON

TIME FOR A HAIR CUT

When they were eighteen, Athenian youths had their hair cut off in a special ceremony. After the ceremony they were known as *ephebes* and it was time to start their two years compulsory training in the army or navy. In Athens the foreigners who lived there, called *metics*, had to join up as well. Slaves were the only ones who were let off.

MAYBE THERE'S SOME GOOD IN BEING A SLAVE AFTER ALL!

RUN! EYES LEFT! SPEARS UP! ON THE DOUBLE! YOU 'ORRIBLE LITTLE MAN, CLEON! RUN!!

HOPLITE? HOPHEAVY MORE LIKE!

The tanks of Ancient Greek armies were heavily armed men called *hoplites* fighting close together in a group of men called a *phalanx*. The lines of a phalanx were usually eight men deep although later phalanxes could be as much as fifty men deep. The men stood about a shield's width apart and the spears of the back lines often jutted past the men in the front line in a sort of hedgehog-prickle effect.

THE MACEDONIAN PHALANX

CRESTED HELMET

SPEAR

WOOD AND BRONZE SHIELD, OR HOPLON. SOMETIMES PAINTED WITH THE 'EVIL EYE' — TO WARD OFF BAD LUCK

GET A MOVE ON, SLAVE! WE'VE GOT A WAR TO FIGHT!

SHOULDER YOKES

I KNEW IT WAS TOO GOOD TO LAST!

BODY PROTECTOR, CALLED A CUIRASS. MADE OF BRONZE OR STIFF CANVAS

PUFF! YESSIR! PANT!

HOPLITES ON CAMPAIGN OFTEN HAD A SLAVE TO CARRY FOOD, WATER AND WEAPONS

SWORD IN SCABBARD

BRONZE LEG — ARMOUR, CALLED GREAVES

TOUGH SANDALS

HOPLITE, c. 480 BC

Phalanxes were made up of citizens who were rich enough to afford armour. Poorer citizens joined the navy as oarsmen or became *peltasts*, lightly armed troops who fought with slings or spears.

PERSIAN PERIL!

Darius I 522-486 BC King of Persia built the mightiest empire ever seen till then. It stretched from India to the Mediterranean.

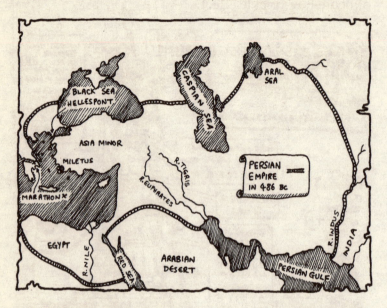

Darius had hardly heard of the Greeks, apart from a few piffling cities under his rule along the Mediterranean coast of Asia Minor (cities which included Miletus, the home of philosophy, among others). Imagine his surprise when in 500 BC those cities declared their independence from his empire, and the Athenians backed the rebels up. 'Athenians,' said the mighty emperor, 'who are they?'

He was about to find out.

Check out these sensational snippets.

GREEK WEEKLY

494 BC
DARIUS DASHES FREE DREAM

Persian Emperor Darius has defeated the rebellious Greek cities of Asia Minor in a sea battle at Lade. Miletus, home of many of our greatest philosophers, has been conquered and reports suggest that it will never recover.

491 BC
ATHENS BEWARE!

Reports have reached us that Darius has collected an army of 100,000 men and intends to send them by sea to conquer the cities of mainland Greece. He is understood to be very keen to teach the Athenians a lesson.

490 BC
PANIC!

We regret to report that many Greek cities have made peace with the Persian invaders. Others such as the Spartans have delayed sending their armies to help the Athenians. Only the brave Athenians and the Plataeans are ready to fight. The Athenian leader Miltiades has enlisted slaves as well as citizens and promised them their freedom.

490 BC
GOTCHA!

10,000 Athenians and Plataeans have smashed 100,000 Persians on the plain of *Marathon*. 6,400 Persians have been killed and only 192 of our own brave boys.

You can still see the grave mound of the Greek soldiers on the plain of Marathon.

482 BC
PERSIAN PERIL PART 2

Persian Emperor Xerxes is said to be getting ready for another attack on our dear homeland. The new Persian army is 200,000 strong. Remember what happened to your father's army, Xerxes!

481 BC
BOAT BRIDGE

Xerxes' army has crossed the narrow strip of sea between Europe and Asia, the Hellespont. Reports say that Xerxes built a bridge of 674 ships, lashed together in two rows and covered in wooden planks and earth. Eyewitnesses report that it took seven days and nights for his enormous army to cross.

480 BC
SPARTAN HEROES

A Greek army of 4,000, led by the Spartans, has held back the Persians at a pass through the mountains north of Athens called *Thermopylae*. They are said to have fought with extreme bravery but have been defeated by the massive Persian force. Athens is now helpless before the invaders.

Darius died in 486 BC. Xerxes' army was so big that if it ate more than two meals in one city, that city ran out of food and was ruined.

RUNNING THE MARATHON

In 490 BC just before the Battle of Marathon, Pheidippides ran from Athens to Sparta, a distance of roughly 260 kilometres, to ask for help. The Spartans had a religious festival and refused to set off until it was over, so he ran back to Athens - a total of 520 kilometres.

However the race called 'marathon' gets its name from the feat of another man who ran the 44 kilometres from Marathon to Athens, having fought in the battle. He brought news of the victory then dropped down dead. It's a good thing that the modern Marathon is based on this run and not on the 520 kilometres of Pheidippides!

THE THREE HUNDRED

At the Battle of Thermopylae in 480 BC, twenty thousand out of the Persian army of two hundred thousand were killed - but only three hundred Greeks died even though they lost the battle. This was because Leonidas, King of the Spartans, together with three hundred Spartan warriors, defended the pass against the entire Persian army while the rest of the Greeks slipped away. Nearly all Leonidas' three hundred died where they fought.

300 v. 200,000 = not bad going, even for a phalanx of Spartan hoplites.

RAMMED!

SHIPS, AND EMPIRES OF THE SEA

ALL ABOARD - WELL ALMOST

Athens lay helpless before the Persian army like a mole hill before a motor mower, just waiting to be squashed. The Athenians faced death or slavery. They had to get out - and fast.

Luckily they had a brand new fleet of two hundred warships. In 482, only two years before, a new rich vein of silver had been found in the silver mines of Laurium. *Themistocles*, one of their leaders, had persuaded them to spend their new wealth on ships rather than luxuries.

They scrambled to the port of Piraeus with whatever they could carry. Once they were all on board almost the entire population of Athens sailed across the sea to camp on nearby coasts. When Xerxes entered the city it was as good as deserted.

WHERE ARE THOSE GREEK DOGS?

SIRE - THEY ARE ALL ROUND THE PORT, HOWLING AND BARKING!

NOT THOSE DOGS, YOU BLOCKHEAD!

The ancient writer Plutarch describes how pets followed their families to the port and howled when they were not allowed to board the ships with them.

Trireme

Most Greek warships were triremes. These were war galleys rowed by 170 oarsmen probably sitting in three banks on either side. The oarsmen were free citizens and were paid a daily rate.

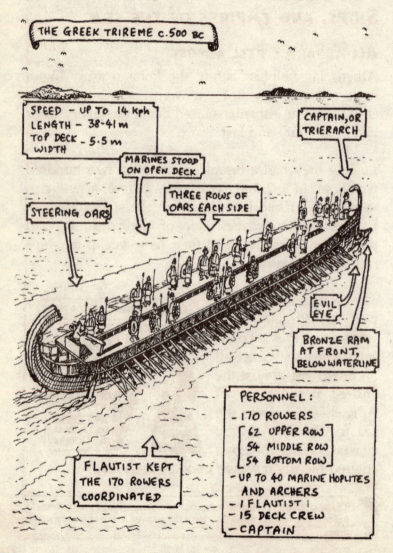

THE GREEK TRIREME c.500 BC

SPEED – UP TO 14 Kph
LENGTH – 38-41 m
TOP DECK
WIDTH – 5.5 m

CAPTAIN, OR TRIERARCH

MARINES STOOD ON OPEN DECK

THREE ROWS OF OARS EACH SIDE

STEERING OARS

EVIL EYE

BRONZE RAM AT FRONT, BELOW WATERLINE

FLAUTIST KEPT THE 170 ROWERS COORDINATED

PERSONNEL:
- 170 ROWERS
  [62 UPPER ROW
   54 MIDDLE ROW
   54 BOTTOM ROW]
- UP TO 40 MARINE HOPLITES AND ARCHERS
- 1 FLAUTIST
- 15 DECK CREW
- CAPTAIN

RATHER A LARGE ROWING BOAT

In the second century BC the philosopher and scientist Archimedes designed a massive ship for Hieron, tyrant of Syracuse. The ship needed six hundred oarsmen and could carry three hundred passengers or soldiers in sixty cabins, some with mosaic floors and ivory doors.

Great beams jutted from its eight armoured turrets. They had holes in the end so that stones could be dropped on enemy ships. It also had a massive catapult to hurl huge stones or arrows up to five metres long. For comfort it had a short sports stadium, a large marble bath and a shady deck-garden with plants.

It was too expensive to run, so Hieron filled it with corn and fish and sent it as a present to Egypt which was suffering from a famine at the time.

TRIREME TACTICS

Triremes had two basic tactics and some fancy ones:

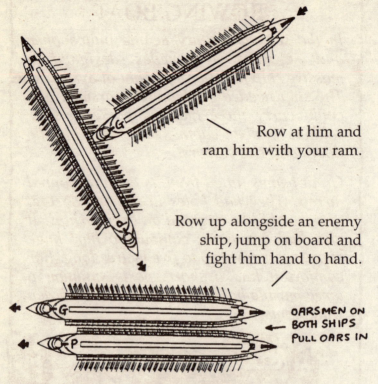

Row at him and
ram him with your ram.

Row up alongside an enemy
ship, jump on board and
fight him hand to hand.

OARSMEN ON
BOTH SHIPS
PULL OARS IN

One fancy tactic was to row alongside an enemy ship
and then pull in your oars as your trireme surged past.
The side of your ship then broke all the enemy oars on
one side and left him helpless.

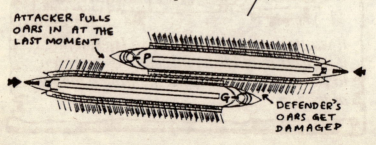

ATTACKER PULLS
OARS IN AT THE
LAST MOMENT

DEFENDER'S
OARS GET
DAMAGED

SALAMIS

I MUST SMASH THOSE GREEK DOGS! BUT HOW??

ON XERXES' SHIP...

SIRE — YOUR FLEET IS THE BIGGER—FIGHT THEM AT THE BAY OF SALAMIS! THEY WILL BE TRAPPED THERE!

As well as a vast army, Xerxes had started out with a fleet of a thousand ships. He needed the fleet to bring food to his army, because the army ate more than could be gathered from the poor countryside of Greece. Without the fleet to supply it, his army would starve.

Having dumped the Athenian refugees on the coast, crafty Themistocles, now the Greek commander, lured the Persian fleet into a narrow stretch of water in the bay of Salamis. He had just three hundred Greek triremes to fight the massive Persian fleet, but he had made sure that the Persian ships had no room to fight properly.

AT THE GREEK CAMP...

WE'LL FIGHT THEM AT THE BAY OF SALAMIS! WE CAN TRAP THEM THERE!

GREAT IDEA, THEMISTOCLES!

OH NO!..

SIRE — WE ARE DEFEATED!

DEATH!

BUT SIRE...

DEATH!!

Xerxes watched the battle from a throne on the shore.

The Persians were smashed to pieces. It was time for Xerxes to go home.

FEELING MIFFED?

Greek myths part 4
Odysseus's odd adventures

Homer's Odyssey tells how Odysseus and his companions sailed home from the Trojan War. They went the long way round and had a lot of adventures. Meanwhile back home in Ithaca Odysseus' faithful wife Penelope tried to fend off lots of men who wanted to marry her while he was away.

Odysseus' adventures included:

Freeing his men from a one-eyed giant who had imprisoned them. He used a stake to strike the giant in the eye!

Befriending the sorceress Circe who had changed all his men into animals. (She changed them back again.)

Losing eleven of his twelve ships when a bunch of cannibal giants threw rocks at them!

Sailing past the sirens who tried to lure them towards some dangerous rocks by singing sweetly.

Odysseus arrived home at last and killed all the men who were trying to marry Penelope.

League temples

After the Battle of Salamis Athens was cock of the walk, she was prize pig in the pigsty, she was fastest racehorse on the track. She had defeated the Persians at Salamis and Marathon almost single handed. All the other Greek cities had her to thank for their freedom.

The Athenians formed the 'Delian League' in 477 BC which was meant to be a group of free cities getting together for their own safety and trade. But it soon turned into an Athenian *empire* because Athens had most of the ships and all the real power. Money from the other cities in the league flowed into the treasure chests of Athens. This money paid for the temple of the Parthenon and other beautiful buildings started by the new Athenian leader, Pericles.

Pericles was a democrat at home - but an empire builder abroad. He did everything he could to make Athens as rich and powerful as possible.

As far as other Greek cities were concerned, Athens was definitely prize pig in the pigsty - she'd got her snout in the trough and she was gobbling up all the pig food!

The staircase to suicide

Some of the other cities turned to Sparta for help. Sparta had never been a part of the Delian League.

Soon the whole of Greece was on the side of either Sparta or Athens. It was the start of a bloody civil war called the *Peloponnesian War* which lasted from 431-404 BC. It ruined everybody.

Lots of horrible things went on during the Peloponnesian War. The historian Thucydides kept a day to day record of it all. For much of the time the Athenians were trapped within their city and could only get in and out by sea through the port of Piraeus which was connected to the city by thirteen kilometres of 'Long Walls'. Here are a few of the main events:

SEEK OUT THE GREEK PART 5

Would you make a hard hoplite?
(Answers on page 122)

1. YOU'RE OUT ON CAMPAIGN. YOU HAVE A LOT OF HEAVY BAGGAGE. DO YOU ?..

a Leave some of it at home
b Get a slave to carry it
c Carry it yourself

2. THE ENEMY IS LINED UP AND READY FOR BATTLE. DO YOU ?..

a Charge forward, pick on the first man you can see and engage him in single combat
b Tell your commander you've got a headache and you need to sit down for a while
c Form a close formation with your comrades and march together towards the enemy

3. WHAT IS YOUR FAVOURITE WEAPON?

a A great big club with nails in it
b A thrusting spear
c A throwing javelin

103

Thirty shirty tyrants - and life after death

The Spartans gave control of Athens to thirty rich Athenians. The 'Thirty' executed 1,500 democrats and exiled another 5,000. Times were tough.

However Athens was down - but not out. Before long the 'Thirty' were booted out and democracy restored. Even so, the city would never get its empire back, and the Greek cities would never be truly free again.

But a new golden age was just round the corner. And Athens, being Athens, would be at the centre of it.

To HELL'N BACK

Hellenistic pages

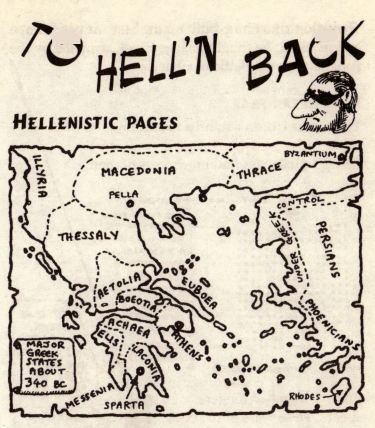

A map of the major Greek states about 340 BC, labelled with: ILLYRIA, MACEDONIA, PELLA, THRACE, BYZANTIUM, THESSALY, UNDER GREEK CONTROL, PERSIANS, AETOLIA, BOEOTIA, EUBOEA, PHOENICIANS, ACHAEA, ELIS, ATHENS, LACONIA, MESSENIA, SPARTA, RHODES.

MAJOR GREEK STATES ABOUT 340 BC

Mad Macedonian number 1

Philip II of Macedon was a one-eyed wonder. He lost the other eye in a fight. Due to fighting he also had a broken shoulder, a paralysed arm and a limp. His kingdom of Macedonia lay just to the north of Greece. He and his people spoke Greek, although true Greeks didn't think that Macedonians were Greek at all.

Not that Philip cared what they thought. He liked the Greeks and he was going to unify the Greek cities under his own leadership whether they agreed with him or not.

105

They didn't. So Philip built up the best army in Europe and in 338 BC he fought a large Greek army led by the Athenians at the Battle of Chaeronea.

REAR SPEAR FEAR

The 'Greeks' didn't stand a chance.

Philip's phalanxes had more rows of men.

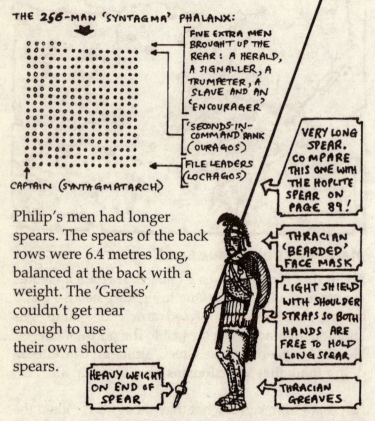

THE 256-MAN 'SYNTAGMA' PHALANX:

FIVE EXTRA MEN BROUGHT UP THE REAR: A HERALD, A SIGNALLER, A TRUMPETER, A SLAVE AND AN 'ENCOURAGER'

'SECONDS-IN-COMMAND' RANK (OURAGOS)

FILE LEADERS (LOCHAGOS)

CAPTAIN (SYNTAGMATARCH)

VERY LONG SPEAR. COMPARE THIS ONE WITH THE HOPLITE SPEAR ON PAGE 89!

THRACIAN 'BEARDED' FACE MASK

LIGHT SHIELD WITH SHOULDER STRAPS SO BOTH HANDS ARE FREE TO HOLD LONG SPEAR

HEAVY WEIGHT ON END OF SPEAR

THRACIAN GREAVES

Philip's men had longer spears. The spears of the back rows were 6.4 metres long, balanced at the back with a weight. The 'Greeks' couldn't get near enough to use their own shorter spears.

It was a walk-over - literally. Luckily for the Greeks, Philip was not a cruel man, and he respected the Athenians.

MAD MACEDONIAN NUMBER 2

Philip was murdered by one of his officers in 336 BC, and his son Alexander III took over.

Alexander had more energy in him than a rocket. He loved danger and even as a commander he always plunged into the thick of a fight. He could mount and dismount from his chariot at full speed. He couldn't bear to rest and on those rare days when he wasn't fighting he would rush off hunting. He even hated to waste time on sleep, and after a hard day's fighting he liked to sit up half the night talking with scholars and scientists.

No wonder he conquered half the known world.

It was Alexander who started the habit of shaving in Europe. He thought whiskers made an easy handle for an enemy to grab hold of.

Alexander was so small that when he sat on the throne of the Emperor of Persia his legs swung freely and a servant had to fetch a stool.

WHO'S YER FATHER?

Alexander's mother Olympias claimed that she was descended from Achilles, the ancient hero of the Trojan War. (Annoyingly for Philip, she also claimed that the god Zeus was Alexander's real father.) Alexander carried a copy of *The Iliad* 🦶 wherever he went. At night he often placed it under his pillow beside his dagger.

So when Alexander invaded Asia in 334 BC he chose to follow the exact path to Troy of his supposed ancestor Achilles, as described in *The Iliad*. At every step he quoted great chunks of *The Iliad* to his companions. He even ran naked round Achilles' tomb as a sign of respect. As far as Alexander was concerned, he was taking up the adventure where the earlier heroes had left off around a thousand years before.

🦶 Homer's famous poem about the Trojan War and heroes like Achilles. See page 14.

Seek out the Greek part 6

How educated are you?

Ancient Greek historians such as Herodotus and Thucydides were the first people to write history books. Now that you've nearly finished this history book, how would you do as an historian?

(Answers on page 122)

1. Who was Darius?

a An Egyptian pharaoh who ruled from 1,500-1,440 BC

b A Persian emperor

c A Persian cat

2. At the Battle of Thermopylae ...

a Xerxes defeated the Greeks

b The Greeks defeated Xerxes

c The Greeks and the Persians fought each other to a standstill, then the Persians went home

3. Reading a book can be a *Marathon*. But what do you know about the *real* Marathon?

a It was a plain where the Greeks defeated the Persians in 490 BC

b It was a race at the Ancient Olympic games

c It was a battle fought between the Spartans and the Athenians in 482 BC

IF IT'S TUESDAY IT MUST BE INDIA

Alexander was a man in a hurry. It took him just ten years to conquer most of the civilized world outside China.

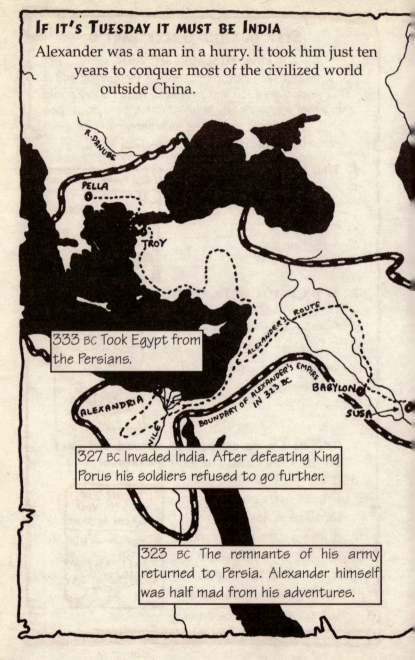

333 BC Took Egypt from the Persians.

327 BC Invaded India. After defeating King Porus his soldiers refused to go further.

323 BC The remnants of his army returned to Persia. Alexander himself was half mad from his adventures.

In 323 BC Alexander and two friends were first to scale the walls of the city of the Indian Mallians - typical of him. The ladders broke and they were cut off alone within the enemy city. Alexander fought till he sank exhausted from his wounds and was only just rescued when the rest of the army broke in.

In his last years Alexander publically declared that he really was a god and the son of Zeus (although to his friends in private Alexander never pretended any such thing). His mother laughed when she heard that he had taken her story about his birth seriously.

CHINA

PERSIANS

KINGDOM OF PORUS

334-330 BC Conquered Persian Empire.

R. INDUS

MULTAN

INDIA

Alexander took to wearing eastern clothes and to drinking heavily. One night in 323 BC he drank seven litres of wine. The next night he drank heavily again, then he caught a fever. His generals asked him to whom he would leave his empire and he replied: 'To the strongest'. Shortly afterwards he died. He was only thirty-three years old.

CRUMBLE JUMBLE

Alexander's empire crumbled to pieces and his top generals grabbed what they could.

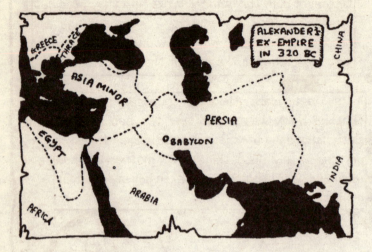

Seleucus selected Persia and Babylon
Ptolemy took Egypt
Antipater grabbed Greece
Antigonus accepted Asia Minor

Thanks to Alexander, the Greeks now ruled huge numbers of other people from India to the Atlantic. *Hellenes* was what the Greeks called themselves and the period of their greatest power is called the *Hellenistic Age*.

PRETTY CITIES

Huge cities grew up in the lands under Greek control. *Syracuse* in Sicily had a population of half a million.

Pronounced *Tollemy*

Alexandria in Egypt had walls twenty-four kilometres long and a population only slightly smaller than Syracuse's. In Alexandria there were shaded colonnades and along the beach front there were bathing resorts. Women of all classes shopped in the stores and mingled freely in the streets.

Greeks, Jews, Egyptians, Persians, Arabs and Africans all lived in Alexandria. Each nationality had its own section of the city, and as in most Hellenistic cities the Greeks kept themselves separate from the 'barbarians'. After all they were the top dogs. In some cities, such as Marseilles, they even built a wall across the town to cut themselves off from the barbarians.

Every national group spoke its own language, but many people spoke Greek as well. It was the international language of its time, just as English is today. Greek ideas and fashions were everywhere. The Jews in Jerusalem built a gymnasium. Jewish priests were horrified at the thought of Jewish youths exercising naked, but what could they do? Greek culture was so much more fun and more exciting than most other cultures.

SPOT THE PARROT

The larger cities had the money to put on huge shows. In 270 BC Alexandria put on a procession in honour of Dionysus . Wine was sloshed on to the streets from huge pitchers and there was limitless free drink. There were statues with limbs that moved, officials dressed as satyrs, 2,000 oxen dressed in gold, 2,400 dogs, ostriches pulling carts, giraffes, elephants, antelopes and a few parrots. How many parrots can you spot in this picture?

Answer ꓸsʇoɹɹɐd ɹnoɟ ǝɹɐ ǝɹǝɥꓕ

See page 38 for more on *Dionysus*.

Book crooks

Greek learning spread with Greek power. The Greek for a book was *biblos*, where our word 'Bible' comes from. Their books were written on long lengths of papyrus and later vellum 👣 and wound up into rolls. Several rolls were needed to make up the length of a medium-sized modern book.

There were huge libraries at Alexandria, Pergamum and other cities. Book collecting became a disease! Rulers fought to build the largest libraries. The Ptolemies of Egypt had it really bad. Their public library at Alexandria was the largest in the world with at least 532,000 books at its peak. All ships entering the harbour of Alexandria were stopped and searched for books. If any were found which were not in the library, they were taken away and copied.

👣 *Vellum* is specially treated smooth leather.

Greek learning wasn't all words in books. Their philosophers kept on thinking and their scientists kept on inventing things. Ctesibius of Alexandria invented a pressure pump and a water organ; his pupil Hero invented a sort of steam machine called an *aeolipile*.

But the Greeks were going to need more than water organs and steam engines which couldn't do anything. A new and very powerful enemy was waiting to pounce.

ROMAN TEMPER

EYPEKA!

NOT THE BEGINNING OF THE END BUT THE END ITSELF

MIND OVER MUSCLE

By 212 BC Rome had grown from a small collection of villages to become the most powerful city in Italy, and the brutal Roman war machine was only just moving into second gear. Greek phalanxes were no match for seriously ruthless Roman legions.

To the south of Italy the rich Greek cities of Sicily sweltered in the sun, like ripe figs waiting to be picked. Syracuse was the largest and richest of them all and Syracuse made the bad mistake of siding with Rome's enemies.

AREA UNDER ROMAN CONTROL IN ABOUT 300 BC BY 200 BC, ALL OF THIS MAP WAS ROMAN

KEY:
UNDER GREEKS
UNDER CARTHAGE
CITIES

CORSICA · ETRUSCANS · ROME · ITALY · ADRIATIC SEA · SARDINIA · NEAPOLIS · TARENTUM · SYBARIS · SICILY · TO GREECE · RHEGIUM · IONIAN SEA · CARTHAGE · SYRACUSE

The Romans attacked with a fleet and an army expecting an easy victory - but they reckoned without Archimedes the philosopher.

DEADLY DESIGNS

Seventy-five-year-old Archimedes designed some amazing war machines:

Vast catapults shot so many stones that the Roman army and some ships could not get near to the city walls.

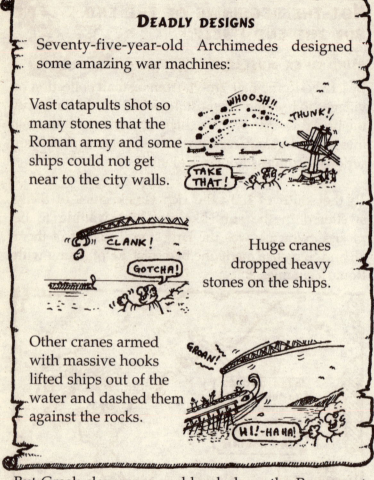

Huge cranes dropped heavy stones on the ships.

Other cranes armed with massive hooks lifted ships out of the water and dashed them against the rocks.

But Greek cleverness could only keep the Romans at bay. Nothing could defeat them. The Romans surrounded Syracuse and after eight months they were able to march into a starving and helpless city. Archimedes was killed by a Roman soldier.

The Roman war machine was quite simply unstoppable. The invaders gobbled up Sicily and then Greece itself. By the 190s it was all over. Along with half the world, the cities of Greece had finally lost their freedom to the conqueror. The Ancient Greeks would never get their freedom back.

IT'S ALL GREEK TO ME

This story doesn't really have an end; in a way it's still going on. The Romans smashed the Greeks, but they were also their number one fans. They loved the Greek way of doing things. They loved it so much that they copied it. What we think of as Roman writing, architecture and painting are all copied from the Greeks. In fact a large part of Roman civilization is one big copy!

That's not the end of it. The Greek way of doing things is like air, it gets everywhere. It has spread over a far wider area than the Roman Empire and over a much longer period of time. Amazingly, all modern civilization is based on ways of thinking which the Ancient Greeks developed nearly three thousand years ago.

They taught us that it's good to have the freedom to question everything and to think for ourselves. From that freedom comes all of modern science, maths, technology, history, sport, art, literature and democracy.

Not bad for a small number of midget cities which were built on the edges of the Mediterranean 'like frogs round a pond' such a very long time ago.

Answers to seek out the Greek

Part 1 You need all of them to be a Greek hero. Score one point if you do.

Part 2 None of them of course. This quiz is to find out if you could have been an Ancient Greek - not a god! One point for the correct answer.

Part 3 1 - b,d,e & f (Zeus won't enjoy using a or eating c, that's for sure.) 2 - a (You'll have taken your test before forty years is up and Zeus won't be impressed by the sink.) A point for each correct answer.

Part 4 1 - a, 2 - b, 3 - a. A point for each correct answer.

Part 5 1 - b, 2 - c, 3 - c. A point for each correct answer.

Part 6 1 - b, 2 - a, 3 - a. A point for each correct answer.

Scores

Under 5	Hopeless - you'd better stay in the twentieth century
5-10	Not bad - for a barbarian
10-16	Eureka! You must have Greek blood in your veins!

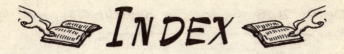

INDEX

WHAT THEY DON'T TELL YOU ABOUT...

Other books in the series

ABOUT THE AUTHOR

Bob Fowke is a prize-winning children's author. He has written (or co-written) over seventy exciting books, from history and science to dinosaurs and spaceships . Bob started off painting book covers for science-fiction and horror stories by famous writers such as HP Lovecraft and Philip K Dick.

Bob is now the editorial advisor at www.youcaxton.co.uk - a company that offers support to Self-Publishers.